Henry Wadsworth Longfellow

In the Harbor

Ultima Thule

Henry Wadsworth Longfellow

In the Harbor
Ultima Thule

ISBN/EAN: 9783744759281

Printed in Europe, USA, Canada, Australia, Japan

Cover: Foto ©ninafisch / pixelio.de

More available books at **www.hansebooks.com**

IN THE HARBOR

ULTIMA THULE.—PART II.

BY

HENRY WADSWORTH LONGFELLOW

" Ultima Thule ! Utmost Isle !
Here in thy harbors for a while
We lower our sails ; a while we rest
From the unending, endless quest "

BOSTON
HOUGHTON, MIFFLIN AND COMPANY
New York: 11 East Seventeenth Street
The Riverside Press, Cambridge
1882

CONTENTS.

———◆———

POEMS.

TRANSLATIONS.

PERSONAL POEMS.

L'ENVOI.

NOTE.

THIS volume contains all of Mr. Longfellow's unprinted poems which will be given to the public, with the exception of two sonnets reserved for his Biography, and "Michael Angelo," a dramatic poem, which will be published later.

"The Children's Crusade" was left unfinished. It is founded upon an event which occurred in the year 1212. An army of twenty thousand children, mostly boys, under the lead of a boy of ten years, named Nicolas, set out from Cologne for the Holy Land. When they reached Genoa only seven thousand remained.

There, as the sea did not divide to allow them to march dry-shod to the East, they broke up. Some got as far as Rome; two ship-loads sailed from Pisa, and were not heard of again; the rest straggled back to Germany.

POEMS.

BECALMED.

BECALMED upon the sea of Thought,
Still unattained the land it sought,
My mind, with loosely-hanging sails,
Lies waiting the auspicious gales.

On either side, behind, before,
The ocean stretches like a floor, —
A level floor of amethyst,
Crowned by a golden dome of mist.

Blow, breath of inspiration, blow!
Shake and uplift this golden glow!
And fill the canvas of the mind
With wafts of thy celestial wind.

Blow, breath of song! until I feel
The straining sail, the lifting keel,
The life of the awakening sea,
Its motion and its mystery!

HERMES TRISMEGISTUS.

As Seleucus narrates, Hermes described the principles that rank as wholes in two myriads of books; or, as we are informed by Manetho, he perfectly unfolded these principles in three myriads six thousand five hundred and twenty-five volumes. . . .

. . . Our ancestors dedicated the inventions of their wisdom to this deity, inscribing all their own writings with the name of Hermes. — IAMBLICUS.

STILL through Egypt's desert places
    Flows the lordly Nile,
From its banks the great stone faces
    Gaze with patient smile.
Still the pyramids imperious
    Pierce the cloudless skies,
And the Sphinx stares with mysterious,
    Solemn, stony eyes.

But where are the old Egyptian
    Demi-gods and kings?

Nothing left but an inscription
 Graven on stones and rings.
Where are Helius and Hephoestus,
 Gods of eldest eld?
Where is Hermes Trismegistus,
 Who their secrets held?

Where are now the many hundred
 Thousand books he wrote?
By the Thaumaturgists plundered,
 Lost in lands remote;
In oblivion sunk forever,
 As when o'er the land
Blows a storm-wind, in the river
 Sinks the scattered sand.

Something unsubstantial, ghostly,
 Seems this Theurgist,
In deep meditation mostly
 Wrapped, as in a mist.

Vague, phantasmal, and unreal
 To our thought he seems,
Walking in a world ideal,
 In a land of dreams.

Was he one, or many, merging
 Name and fame in one,
Like a stream, to which, converging,
 Many streamlets run?
Till, with gathered power proceeding,
 Ampler sweep it takes,
Downward the sweet waters leading
 From unnumbered lakes.

By the Nile I see him wandering,
 Pausing now and then,
On the mystic union pondering
 Between gods and men;
Half believing, wholly feeling,
 With supreme delight,

How the gods, themselves concealing,
    Lift men to their height.

Or in Thebes, the hundred-gated,
    In the thoroughfare
Breathing, as if consecrated,
    A diviner air;
And amid discordant noises,
    In the jostling throng,
Hearing far, celestial voices
    Of Olympian song.

Who shall call his dreams fallacious?
    Who has searched or sought
All the unexplored and spacious
    Universe of thought?
Who, in his own skill confiding,
    Shall with rule and line
Mark the border-land dividing
    Human and divine?

Trismegistus! three times greatest!
    How thy name sublime,
Has descended to this latest
    Progeny of time!
Happy they whose written pages
    Perish with their lives,
If amid the crumbling ages
    Still their name survives!

Thine, O priest of Egypt, lately
    Found I in the vast,
Weed-encumbered, sombre, stately,
    Grave-yard of the Past;
And a presence moved before me
    On that gloomy shore,
As a waft of wind, that o'er me
    Breathed, and was no more.

THE POET'S CALENDAR.

JANUARY.

I.

JANUS am I; oldest of potentates;
 Forward I look, and backward, and below
I count, as god of avenues and gates,
 The years that through my portals come
 and go.

II.

I block the roads, and drift the fields with
 snow;
 I chase the wild-fowl from the frozen fen;
My frosts congeal the rivers in their flow,
 My fires light up the hearths and hearts of
 men.

FEBRUARY.

I am lustration; and the sea is mine!
  I wash the sands and headlands with my
    tide;
My brow is crowned with branches of the
    pine;
  Before my chariot-wheels the fishes glide.
By me all things unclean are purified,
  By me the souls of men washed white again;
E'en the unlovely tombs of those who died
  Without a dirge, I cleanse from every stain.

MARCH.

I Martius am! Once first, and now the
    third!
  To lead the Year was my appointed place;
A mortal dispossessed me by a word,
  And set there Janus with the double face.

Hence I make war on all the human race;
  I shake the cities with my hurricanes;
I flood the rivers and their banks efface,
  And drown the farms and hamlets with my
    rains.

APRIL.

I open wide the portals of the Spring
  To welcome the procession of the flowers,
With their gay banners, and the birds that
    sing
  Their song of songs from their aerial tow-
    ers.
I soften with my sunshine and my showers
  The heart of earth; with thoughts of love
    I glide
Into the hearts of men; and with the hours
  Upon the Bull with wreathèd horns I ride.

MAY.

Hark !   The sea-faring wild-fowl loud proclaim
  My coming, and the swarming of the bees.
These are my heralds, and behold ! my name
  Is written in blossoms on the hawthorn-
      trees.
I tell the mariner when to sail the seas;
  I waft o'er all the land from far away
The breath and bloom of the Hesperides,
  My birthplace. I am Maia. I am May.

JUNE.

Mine is the Month of Roses ; yes, and mine
  The Month of Marriages !   All pleasant
      sights
And scents, the fragrance of the blossoming
      vine,
  The foliage of the valleys and the heights.

Mine are the longest days, the loveliest nights ;
  The mower's scythe makes music to my ear ;
I am the mother of all dear delights ;
  I am the fairest daughter of the year.

JULY.

My emblem is the Lion, and I breathe
  The breath of Libyan deserts o'er the land ;
My sickle as a sabre I unsheathe,
  And bent before me the pale harvests stand.
The lakes and rivers shrink at my command,
  And there is thirst and fever in the air ;
The sky is changed to brass, the earth to
      sand ;
  I am the Emperor whose name I bear.

AUGUST.

The Emperor Octavian, called the August,
  I being his favorite, bestowed his name
Upon me, and I hold it still in trust,
  In memory of him and of his fame.
I am the Virgin, and my vestal flame
  Burns less intensely than the Lion's rage;
Sheaves are my only garlands, and I claim
  The golden Harvests as my heritage.

SEPTEMBER.

I bear the Scales, where hang in equipoise
  The night and day; and when unto my lips
I put my trumpet, with its stress and noise
  Fly the white clouds like tattered sails of
    ships;
The tree-tops lash the air with sounding
    whips;

2

Southward the clamorous sea-fowl wing their
    flight;
The hedges are all red with haws and hips,
    The Hunter's Moon reigns empress of the
    night.

OCTOBER.

My ornaments are fruits; my garments leaves,
    Woven like cloth of gold, and crimson dyed;
I do not boast the harvesting of sheaves,
    O'er orchards and o'er vineyards I preside.
Though on the frigid Scorpion I ride,
    The dreamy air is full, and overflows
With tender memories of the summer-tide,
    And mingled voices of the doves and crows

NOVEMBER.

The Centaur, Sagittarius, am I,
    Born of Ixion's and the cloud's embrace;

With sounding hoofs across the earth I fly,
　A steed Thessalian with a human face.
Sharp winds the arrows are with which I
　　chase
　The leaves, half dead already with affright;
I shroud myself in gloom; and to the race
　Of mortals bring nor comfort nor delight.

DECEMBER.

Riding upon the Goat, with snow-white hair,
　I come, the last of all.　This crown of mine
Is of the holly; in my hand I bear
　The thyrsus, tipped with fragrant cones of
　　pine.
I celebrate the birth of the Divine,
　And the return of the Saturnian reign; —
My songs are carols sung at every shrine,
　Proclaiming " Peace on earth, good will to
　　men."

MAD RIVER,

IN THE WHITE MOUNTAINS.

TRAVELLER.

WHY dost thou wildly rush and roar,
Mad River, O Mad River?
Wilt thou not pause and cease to pour
Thy hurrying, headlong waters o'er
This rocky shelf forever?

What secret trouble stirs thy breast?
Why all this fret and flurry?
Dost thou not know that what is best
In this too restless world is rest
From over-work and worry?

THE RIVER.

What wouldst thou in these mountains seek,
　　O stranger from the city?
Is it perhaps some foolish freak
Of thine, to put the words I speak
　　Into a plaintive ditty?

TRAVELLER.

Yes; I would learn of thee thy song,
　　With all its flowing numbers,
And in a voice as fresh and strong
As thine is, sing it all day long,
　　And hear it in my slumbers.

THE RIVER.

A brooklet nameless and unknown
　　Was I at first, resembling
A little child, that all alone
Comes venturing down the stairs of stone,
　　Irresolute and trembling.

Later, by wayward fancies led,
    For the wide world I panted;
Out of the forest dark and dread
Across the open fields I fled,
    Like one pursued and haunted.

I tossed my arms, I sang aloud,
    My voice exultant blending
With thunder from the passing cloud,
The wind, the forest bent and bowed,
    The rush of rain descending.

I heard the distant ocean call,
    Imploring and entreating;
Drawn onward, o'er this rocky wall
I plunged, and the loud waterfall
    Made answer to the greeting.

And now, beset with many ills,
    A toilsome life I follow;

Compelled to carry from the hills
These logs to the impatient mills
    Below there in the hollow.

Yet something ever cheers and charms
    The rudeness of my labors;
Daily I water with these arms
The cattle of a hundred farms,
    And have the birds for neighbors.

Men call me Mad, and well they may,
    When, full of rage and trouble,
I burst my banks of sand and clay,
And sweep their wooden bridge away,
    Like withered reeds or stubble.

Now go and write thy little rhyme,
    As of thine own creating.
Thou seest the day is past its prime;
I can no longer waste my time;
    The mills are tired of waiting.

AUF WIEDERSEHEN.

IN MEMORY OF J. T. F.

UNTIL we meet again! That is the mean-
    ing
Of the familiar words, that men repeat
    At parting in the street.
Ah yes, till then! but when death interven-
    ing
Rends us asunder, with what ceaseless pain
    We wait for the Again!

The friends who leave us do not feel the
    sorrow
Of parting, as we feel it, who must stay
    Lamenting day by day,

And knowing, when we wake upon the mor-
    row,
We shall not find in its accustomed place
    The one beloved face.

It were a double grief, if the departed,
Being released from earth, should still retain
    A sense of earthly pain;
It were a double grief, if the true-hearted,
Who loved us here, should on the farther
    shore
    Remember us no more.

Believing, in the midst of our afflictions,
That death is a beginning, not an end,
    We cry to them, and send
Farewells, that better might be called pre-
    dictions,
Being fore-shadowings of the future, thrown
    Into the vast Unknown.

Faith overleaps the confines of our reason,
And if by faith, as in old times was said,
   Women received their dead
Raised up to life, then only for a season
Our partings are, nor shall we wait in vain
   Until we meet again !

THE CHILDREN'S CRUSADE.

[A FRAGMENT.]

I.

WHAT is this I read in history,
Full of marvel, full of mystery,
Difficult to understand?
Is it fiction, is it truth?
Children in the flower of youth,
Heart in heart, and hand in hand,
Ignorant of what helps or harms,
Without armor, without arms,
Journeying to the Holy Land!

Who shall answer or divine?
Never since the world was made

Such a wonderful crusade
Started forth for Palestine.
Never while the world shall last
Will it reproduce the past;
Never will it see again
Such an army, such a band,
Over mountain, over main,
Journeying to the Holy Land.

Like a shower of blossoms blown
From the parent trees were they;
Like a flock of birds that fly
Through the unfrequented sky,
Holding nothing as their own,
Passed they into lands unknown,
Passed to suffer and to die.

O the simple, child-like trust!
O the faith that could believe
What the harnessed, iron-mailed
Knights of Christendom had failed,

By their prowess, to achieve,
They, the children, could and must!

Little thought the Hermit, preaching
Holy Wars to knight and baron,
That the words dropped in his teaching,
His entreaty, his beseeching,
Would by children's hands be gleaned,
And the staff on which he leaned
Blossom like the rod of Aaron.

As a summer wind upheaves
The innumerable leaves
In the bosom of a wood, —
Not as separate leaves, but massed
All together by the blast, —
So for evil or for good
His resistless breath upheaved
All at once the many-leaved,
Many-thoughted multitude.

3

In the tumult of the air
Rock the boughs with all the nests
Cradled on their tossing crests;
By the fervor of his prayer
Troubled hearts were everywhere
Rocked and tossed in human breasts.

For a century, at least,
His prophetic voice had ceased;
But the air was heated still
By his lurid words and will,
As from fires in far-off woods,
In the autumn of the year,
An unwonted fever broods
In the sultry atmosphere.

II.

In Cologne the bells were ringing,
In Cologne the nuns were singing
Hymns and canticles divine;

Loud the monks sang in their stalls,
And the thronging streets were loud
With the voices of the crowd ; —
Underneath the city walls
Silent flowed the river Rhine.

From the gates, that summer day,
Clad in robes of hodden gray,
With the red cross on the breast,
Azure-eyed and golden-haired,
Forth the young Crusaders fared ;
While above the band devoted
Consecrated banners floated,
Fluttered many a flag and streamer,
And the cross o'er all the rest !
Singing lowly, meekly, slowly,
" Give us, give us back the holy
Sepulchre of the Redeemer ! "
On the vast procession pressed,
Youths and maidens. . . .

III.

Ah! what master hand shall paint
How they journeyed on their way,
How the days grew long and dreary,
How their little feet grew weary,
How their little hearts grew faint!

Ever swifter day by day
Flowed the homeward river; ever
More and more its whitening current
Broke and scattered into spray,
Till the calmly-flowing river
Changed into a mountain torrent,
Rushing from its glacier green
Down through chasm and black ravine.
Like a phœnix in its nest,
Burned the red sun in the West,
Sinking in an ashen cloud;
In the East, above the crest

Of the sea-like mountain chain,
Like a phœnix from its shroud,
Came the red sun back again.

Now around them, white with snow,
Closed the mountain peaks. Below,
Headlong from the precipice
Down into the dark abyss,
Plunged the cataract, white with foam;
And it said, or seemed to say:
" Oh return, while yet you may,
Foolish children, to your home,
There the Holy City is! "

But the dauntless leader said:
" Faint not, though your bleeding feet
O'er these slippery paths of sleet
Move but painfully and slowly;
Other feet than yours have bled;
Other tears than yours been shed.

Courage ! lose not heart or hope ;
On the mountains' southern slope
Lies Jerusalem the Holy ! ''
As a white rose in its pride,
By the wind in summer-tide
Tossed and loosened from the branch,
Showers its petals o'er the ground,
From the distant mountain's side,
Scattering all its snows around,
With mysterious, muffled sound,
Loosened, fell the avalanche.
Voices, echoes far and near,
Roar of winds and waters blending,
Mists uprising, clouds impending,
Filled them with a sense of fear,
Formless, nameless, never ending.

* * * * * *

THE CITY AND THE SEA.

THE panting City cried to the Sea,
"I am faint with heat, — O breathe on me!"

And the Sea said, " Lo, I breathe! but my breath
To some will be life, to others death!"

As to Prometheus, bringing ease
In pain, come the Oceanides,

So to the City, hot with the flame
Of the pitiless sun, the east wind came.

It came from the heaving breast of the deep,
Silent as dreams are, and sudden as sleep.

Life-giving, death-giving, which will it be;
O breath of the merciful, merciless Sea?

SUNDOWN.

THE summer sun is sinking low;
Only the tree-tops redden and glow:
Only the weathercock on the spire
Of the neighboring church is a flame of fire;
    All is in shadow below.

O beautiful, awful summer day,
What hast thou given, what taken away?
Life and death, and love and hate,
Homes made happy or desolate,
    Hearts made sad or gay!

On the road of life one mile-stone more!
In the book of life one leaf turned o'er!
Like a red seal is the setting sun
On the good and the evil men have done, —
    Naught can to-day restore!

July 24, 1879.

PRESIDENT GARFIELD.

"E VENNI DAL MARTIRIO A QUESTA PACE."

THESE words the poet heard in Paradise,
　Uttered by one who, bravely dying here,
　In the true faith was living in that sphere
　Where the celestial cross of sacrifice
Spread its protecting arms athwart the skies;
　And set thereon, like jewels crystal clear,
　The souls magnanimous, that knew not fear,
　Flashed their effulgence on his dazzled eyes.
Ah me! how dark the discipline of pain,
　Were not the suffering followed by the
　　sense
　Of infinite rest and infinite release!
This is our consolation; and again
　A great soul cries to us in our suspense,
　" I came from martyrdom unto this peace!"

DECORATION DAY.

SLEEP, comrades, sleep and rest
  On this Field of the Grounded Arms,
Where foes no more molest,
  Nor sentry's shot alarms!

Ye have slept on the ground before,
  And started to your feet
At the cannon's sudden roar,
  Or the drum's redoubling beat.

But in this camp of Death
  No sound your slumber breaks;
Here is no fevered breath,
  No wound that bleeds and aches.

All is repose and peace,
  Untrampled lies the sod ;
The shouts of battle cease,
  It is the Truce of God !

Rest, comrades, rest and sleep !
  The thoughts of men shall be
As sentinels to keep
  Your rest from danger free.

Your silent tents of green
  We deck with fragrant flowers ;
Yours has the suffering been,
  The memory shall be ours.

February, 3, 1882.

CHIMES.

Sweet chimes! that in the loneliness of night
  Salute the passing hour, and in the dark
  And silent chambers of the household mark
  The movements of the myriad orbs of light!
Through my closed eyelids, by the inner
      sight,
  I see the constellations in the arc
  Of their great circles moving on, and hark!
  I almost hear them singing in their flight.
Better than sleep it is to lie awake
  O'er-canopied by the vast starry dome
  Of the immeasurable sky; to feel
The slumbering world sink under us, and
      make
  Hardly an eddy, — a mere rush of foam
  On the great sea beneath a sinking keel.

    August 28, 1879.

FOUR BY THE CLOCK.

FOUR by the clock! and yet not day;
But the great world rolls and wheels away,
With its cities on land, and its ships at sea,·
Into the dawn that is to be!

Only the lamp in the anchored bark
Sends its glimmer across the dark,
And the heavy breathing of the sea
Is the only sound that comes to me.

NAHANT, *September* 8, 1880,
four o'clock in the morning.

THE FOUR LAKES OF MADISON.

FOUR limpid lakes, — four Naiades
Or sylvan deities are these,
   In flowing robes of azure dressed;
Four lovely handmaids, that uphold
Their shining mirrors, rimmed with gold,
   To the fair city in the West.

By day the coursers of the sun
Drink of these waters as they run
   Their swift diurnal round on high;
By night the constellations glow
Far down the hollow deeps below,
   And glimmer in another sky.

Fair lakes, serene and full of light,
Fair town, arrayed in robes of white,
  How visionary ye appear!
All like a floating landscape seems
In cloud-land or the land of dreams,
  Bathed in a golden atmosphere!

MOONLIGHT.

As a pale phantom with a lamp
  Ascends some ruin's haunted stair,
So glides the moon along the damp
  Mysterious chambers of the air.

Now hidden in cloud, and now revealed,
  As if this phantom, full of pain,
Were by the crumbling walls concealed,
  And at the windows seen again.

Until at last, serene and proud
  In all the splendor of her light,
She walks the terraces of cloud,
  Supreme as Empress of the Night.

I look, but recognize no more
    Objects familiar to my view;
The very pathway to my door
    Is an enchanted avenue.

All things are changed. One mass of shade,
    The elm-trees drop their curtains down;
By palace, park, and colonnade
    I walk as in a foreign town.

The very ground beneath my feet
    Is clothed with a diviner air;
White marble paves the silent street
    And glimmers in the empty square.

Illusion! Underneath there lies
    The common life of every day;
Only the spirit glorifies
    With its own tints the sober gray.

4

In vain we look, in vain uplift
  Our eyes to heaven, if we are blind;
We see but what we have the gift
  Of seeing; what we bring we find.

December 20, 1878.

TO THE AVON.

FLOW on, sweet river! like his verse
Who lies beneath this sculptured hearse;
Nor wait beside the churchyard wall
For him who cannot hear thy call.

Thy playmate once; I see him now
A boy with sunshine on his brow,
And hear in Stratford's quiet street
The patter of his little feet.

I see him by thy shallow edge
Wading knee-deep amid the sedge;
And lost in thought, as if thy stream
Were the swift river of a dream.

He wonders whitherward it flows;
And fain would follow where it goes,
To the wide world, that shall erelong
Be filled with his melodious song.

Flow on, fair stream! That dream is o'er;
He stands upon another shore;
A vaster river near him flows,
And still he follows where it goes.

ELEGIAC VERSE.

I.

PERADVENTURE of old, some bard in Ionian
    Islands,
    Walking alone by the sea, hearing the wash
      of the waves,
Learned the secret from them of the beautiful
    verse elegiac,
    Breathing into his song motion and sound
      of the sea.

For as a wave of the sea, upheaving in long
    undulations,
    Plunges loud on the sands, pauses, and turns,
      and retreats,

So the Hexameter, rising and sinking, with
  cadence sonorous,
Falls; and in refluent rhythm back the Pentameter flows.[1]

II.

Not in his youth alone, but in age, may the
  heart of the poet
Bloom into song, as the gorse blossoms in
  autumn and spring.

III.

Not in tenderness wanting, yet rough are the
  rhymes of our poet;
Though it be Jacob's voice, Esau's, alas!
  are the hands.

---

[1] Compare Schiller.

Im Hexameter steigt des Springquells flüssige Säule;
Im Pentameter drauf fällt sie melodisch herab.

See also Coleridge's translation.

IV.

Let us be grateful to writers for what is left
   in the inkstand;
  When to leave off is an art only attained
   by the few.

V.

How can the Three be One? you ask me; I
   answer by asking,
  Hail and snow and rain, are they not three,
   and yet one?

VI.

By the mirage uplifted the land floats vague
   in the ether,
  Ships and the shadows of ships hang in the
   motionless air;
So by the art of the poet our common life
   is uplifted,
  So, transfigured, the world floats in a lumi-
   nous haze.

VII.

Like a French poem is **Life**; being only per-
fect in structure
When with the masculine rhymes mingled
the feminine are.

VIII.

Down from the mountain descends the brooklet, rejoicing in freedom;
Little it dreams of the mill hid in the val-
ley below;
Glad with the joy of existence, the child goes
singing and laughing,
Little dreaming what toils lie in the future
concealed.

IX.

As the ink from our pen, so flow our thoughts
and our feelings
When we begin to write, however sluggish
before.

X.

Like the Kingdom of Heaven, the Fountain
of Youth is within us ;
If we seek it elsewhere, old shall we grow
in the search.

XI.

If you would hit the mark, you must aim a
little above it ;
Every arrow that flies feels the attraction
of earth.

XII.

Wisely the Hebrews admit no Present tense
in their language :
While we are speaking the word, it is already the Past.

XIII.

In the twilight of age all things seem strange
    and phantasmal,
  As between daylight and dark ghost-like
    the landscape appears.

XIV.

Great is the art of beginning, but greater the
    art is of ending ;
  Many a poem is marred by a superfluous
    verse.

1881.

A FRAGMENT.

AWAKE! arise! the hour is late!
  Angels are knocking at thy door!
They are in haste and cannot wait,
  And once departed come no more.

Awake! arise! the athlete's arm
  Loses its strength by too much rest;
The fallow land, the untilled farm
  Produces only weeds at best.

THE BELLS OF SAN BLAS.[1]

WHAT say the Bells of San Blas
To the ships that southward pass
    From the harbor of Mazatlan?
To them it is nothing more
Than the sound of surf on the shore, —
    Nothing more to master or man.

But to me, a dreamer of dreams,
To whom what is and what seems
    Are often one and the same, —
The Bells of San Blas to me
Have a strange, wild melody,
    And are something more than a name.

[1] The last poem written by Mr. Longfellow.

For bells are the voice of the church;
They have tones that touch and search
    The hearts of young and old;
One sound to all, yet each
Lends a meaning·to their speech,
    And the meaning is manifold.

They are a voice of the Past,
Of an age that is fading fast,
    Of a power austere and grand;
When the flag of Spain unfurled
Its folds o'er this western world,
    And the Priest was lord of the land.

The chapel that once looked down
On the little seaport town
    Has crumbled into the dust;
And on oaken beams below
The bells swing to and fro,
    And are green with mould and rust.

"Is, then, the old faith dead,"
　　They say, "and in its stead
　　　　Is some new faith proclaimed,
　　That we are forced to remain
　　Naked to sun and rain,
　　　　Unsheltered and ashamed?

"Once in our tower aloof
　　We rang over wall and roof
　　　　Our warnings and our complaints;
　　And round about us there
　　The white doves filled the air,
　　　　Like the white souls of the saints.

"The saints! Ah, have they grown
　　Forgetful of their own?
　　　　Are they asleep, or **dead**,
　　That open to the sky
　　Their ruined Missions lie,
　　　　No longer tenanted?

" Oh, bring us back once more
  The vanished days of yore,
      When the world with faith was filled;
Bring back the fervid zeal,
The hearts of fire and steel,
      The hands that believe and build.

" Then from our tower again
  We will send over land and main
      Our voices of command,
Like exiled kings who return
To their thrones, and the people learn
      That the Priest is lord of the land!"

O Bells of San Blas, in vain
Ye call back the Past again!
      The Past is deaf to your prayer:
Out of the shadows of night
The world rolls into light;
      It is daybreak everywhere.

March 15, 1882.

TRANSLATIONS.

PRELUDE.

As treasures that men seek,
  Deep-buried in sea-sands,
Vanish if they but speak,
  And elude their eager hands,

So ye escape and slip,   ·
  O songs, and fade away,
When the word is on my lip
  To interpret what ye say.

Were it not better, then,
  To let the treasures rest
Hid from the eyes of men,
  Locked in their iron chest?

I have but marked the place,
But half the secret told,
That, following this slight trace,
Others may find the gold.

FROM THE FRENCH.

WILL ever the dear days come back again,
  Those days of June, when lilacs were in
    bloom,
  And bluebirds sang their sonnets in the
    gloom
  Of leaves that roofed them in from sun or
    rain?
I know not; but a presence will remain
  Forever and forever in this room,
  Formless, diffused in air, like a perfume, —
  A phantom of the heart, and not the brain.
Delicious days! when every spoken word
  Was like a foot-fall nearer and more near,
  And a mysterious knocking at the gate

Of the heart's secret places, and we heard
  In the sweet tumult of delight and fear
  A voice that whispered, " Open, I cannot
    wait ! "

THE WINE OF JURANÇON.

FROM THE FRENCH OF CHARLES CORAN.

LITTLE sweet wine of Jurançon,
　You are dear to my memory still!
With mine host and his merry song,
　Under the rose-tree I drank my fill.

Twenty years after, passing that way,
　Under the trellis I found again
Mine host, still sitting there *au frais*,
　And singing still the same refrain.

The Jurançon, so fresh and bold,
　Treats me, as one it used to know;
Souvenirs of the days of old
　Already from the bottle flow.

With glass in hand our glances met;
   We pledge, we drink. How sour it is!
Never Argenteuil piquette
   Was to my palate sour as this!

And yet the vintage was good, in sooth;
   The self-same juice, the self-same cask!
It was you, O gayety of my youth,
   That failed in the autumnal flask!

AT LA CHAUDEAU.

FROM THE FRENCH OF XAVIER MARMIER.

AT La Chaudeau, — 't is long since then:
I was young, — my years twice ten;
All things smiled on the happy boy,
ᐧDreams of love and songs of joy,
Azure of heaven and wave below,
  At La Chaudeau.

To La Chaudeau I come back old:
My head is gray, my blood is cold;
Seeking along the meadow ooze,
Seeking beside the river Seymouse,
The days of my spring-time of long ago
  At La Chaudeau.

At La Chaudeau nor heart nor brain
Ever grows old with grief and pain;
A sweet remembrance keeps off age;
A tender friendship doth still assuage
The burden of sorrow that one may know
    At La Chaudeau.

At La Chaudeau, had fate decreed
To limit the wandering life I lead,
Peradventure I still, forsooth,
Should have preserved my fresh green youth,
Under the shadows the hill-tops throw
    At La Chaudeau.

At La Chaudeau, live on, my friends,
Happy to be where God intends;
And sometimes, by the evening fire,
Think of him whose sole desire
Is again to sit in the old château
    At La Chaudeau.

A QUIET LIFE.

FROM THE FRENCH.

LET him who will, by force or fraud innate,
  Of courtly grandeurs gain the slippery
    height;
  I, leaving not the home of my delight,
  Far from the world and noise will medi-
    tate.
Then, without pomps or perils of the great,
  I shall behold the day succeed the night;
  Behold the alternate seasons take their
    flight,
  And in serene repose old age await.
And so, whenever Death shall come to close
  The happy moments that my days compose,
  I, full of years, shall die, obscure, alone!

How wretched is the man, with honors
    crowned,
  Who, having not the one thing needful
    found,
  Dies, known to all, but to himself un-
    known.

September 11, 1879.

PERSONAL POEMS.

LOSS AND GAIN.

WHEN I compare
What I have lost with what I have gained,
What I have missed with what attained,
  Little room do I find for pride.

I am aware
How many days have been idly spent;
How like an arrow the good intent
  Has fallen short or been turned aside.

But who shall dare
To measure loss and gain in this wise?
Defeat may be victory in disguise;
  The lowest ebb is the turn of the tide.

AUTUMN WITHIN.

It is autumn; not without,
  But within me is the cold.
Youth and spring are all about;
  It is I that have grown old.

Birds are darting through the air,
  Singing, building without rest;
Life is stirring everywhere,
  Save within my lonely breast.

There is silence: the dead leaves
  Fall and rustle and are still;
Beats no flail upon the sheaves,
  Comes no murmur from the mill.

April 9, 1874.

VICTOR AND VANQUISHED.

As one who long hath fled with panting breath
  Before his foe, bleeding and near to fall,
  I turn and set my back against the wall,
  And look thee in the face, triumphant
    Death.
I call for aid, and no one answereth;
  I am alone with thee, who conquerest all;
  Yet me thy threatening form doth not ap-
    pall,
  For thou art but a phantom and a wraith.
Wounded and weak, sword broken at the hilt,
  With armor shattered, and without a shield,
  I stand unmoved; do with me what thou
    wilt;
I can resist no more, but will not yield.
  This is no tournament where cowards tilt;
  The vanquished here is victor of the field.

April 4, 1876.

MEMORIES.

OFT I remember those whom I have known
   In other days, to whom my heart was led
   As by a magnet, and who are not dead,
   But absent, and their memories overgrown
With other thoughts and troubles of my own,
   As graves with grasses are, and at their head
   The stone with moss and lichens so o'er-
      spread,
Nothing is legible but the name alone.
And is it so with them? After long years,
   Do they remember me in the same way,
   And is the memory pleasant as to me?
I fear to ask; yet wherefore are my fears?
   Pleasures, like flowers, may wither and de-
      cay,
   And yet the root perennial may be.

September 23, 1881.

MY BOOKS.

SADLY as some old mediæval knight
    Gazed at the arms he could no longer wield,
    The sword two-handed and the shining
        shield
Suspended in the hall, and full in sight,
While secret longings for the lost delight
    Of tourney or adventure in the field
    Came over him, and tears but half concealed
Trembled and fell upon his beard of white,
So I behold these books upon their shelf,
    My ornaments and arms of other days;
    Not wholly useless, though no longer used,
For they remind me of my other self,
    Younger and stronger, and the pleasant
        ways
    In which I walked, now clouded and con-
        fused.

December 27, 1881.

L'ENVOI.

POSSIBILITIES.

WHERE are the Poets, unto whom belong
  The Olympian heights; whose singing shafts
    were sent
  Straight to the mark, and not from bows
    half bent,
  But with the utmost tension of the thong?
Where are the stately argosies of song,
  Whose rushing keels made music as they
    went
  Sailing in search of some new continent,
  With all sail set, and steady winds and
    strong?
Perhaps there lives some dreamy boy, un-
    taught
  In schools, some graduate of the field or
    street,

Who shall become a master of the art,
An admiral sailing the high seas of thought,
   Fearless and first, and steering with his fleet
   For lands not yet laid down in any chart.

January 17, 1882.